Alejandra.

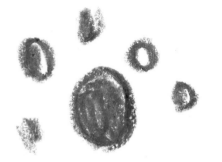

EXPLORE THE U.S.A.

COLORADO

Karen Durrie

LET'S READ
AV2 BY WEIGL™
ADDED VALUE • AUDIO VISUAL

www.av2books.com

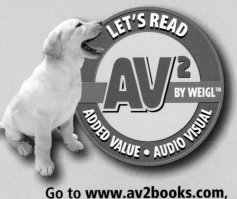

LET'S READ
AV²
BY WEIGL™
ADDED VALUE • AUDIO VISUAL

Go to **www.av2books.com**, and enter this book's unique code.

BOOK CODE

X939034

AV² by Weigl brings you media enhanced books that support active learning.

AV² provides enriched content that supplements and complements this book. Weigl's AV² books strive to create inspired learning and engage young minds in a total learning experience.

Your AV² Media Enhanced books come alive with...

 **Audio**
Listen to sections of the book read aloud.

 **Video**
Watch informative video clips.

Embedded Weblinks
Gain additional information for research.

Try This!
Complete activities and hands-on experiments.

 Key Words
Study vocabulary, and complete a matching word activity.

 Quizzes
Test your knowledge.

 Slide Show
View images and captions, and prepare a presentation.

...and much, much more!

Published by AV² by Weigl
350 5th Avenue, 59th Floor
New York, NY 10118
Website: www.av2books.com   www.weigl.com

Library of Congress Cataloging-in-Publication Data
Durrie, Karen.
 Colorado / Karen Durrie.
   p. cm. -- (Explore the U.S.A.)
 Includes bibliographical references and index.
 ISBN 978-1-61913-331-0 (hard cover : alk. paper)
 1. Colorado--Juvenile literature. I. Title.
 F776.3.D87 2012
 978.8--dc23
                    2012014757

Printed in the United States of America in North Mankato, Minnesota
1 2 3 4 5 6 7 8 9   16 15 14 13 12

052012
WEP040512

Project Coordinator: Karen Durrie
Art Director: Terry Paulhus

Weigl acknowledges Getty Images as the primary image supplier for this title.

COLORADO

Contents

2   AV² Book Code
4   Nickname
6   Location
8   History
10   Flower and Seal
12   Flag
14   Animal
16   Capital
18   Goods
20   Fun Things to Do
22   Facts
24   Key Words

This is Colorado.
It is called Colorful Colorado
for its beautiful mountains, rivers, and plains.

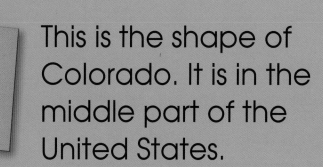

This is the shape of Colorado. It is in the middle part of the United States.

Where is Colorado?

Canada

United States

Pacific Ocean

Atlantic Ocean

Mexico

Colorado is bordered by seven other states.

American Indians made homes in Colorado cliffs thousands of years ago.

The cliff houses were moved more than 100 years ago.

9

The Colorado state flower is the columbine. Hummingbirds and butterflies drink columbine nectar.

The state seal has a pick, an eye, and a sledgehammer.

The pick and the sledgehammer are tools used by miners.

This is the state flag of Colorado. It has a yellow circle and a red C.

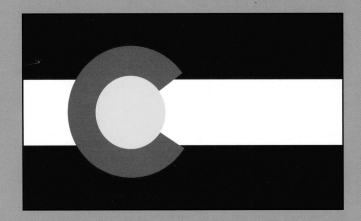

The yellow circle stands for the Sun.

The state animal is the bighorn sheep. Bighorn sheep live in the mountains of Colorado.

Bighorn sheep are very good climbers.

This is the largest city in Colorado. It is named Denver. Denver is the state capital.

Denver has more city parks than any other city in the United States.

Colorado has many cows.
More than two million cows
live in Colorado.

Colorado makes almost
$5 billion each year from
cattle ranching.

Many people go to Colorado to ski. Colorado has 53 mountains that are more than 14,000 feet high.

21

COLORADO FACTS

These pages provide detailed information that expands on the interesting facts found in the book. These pages are intended to be used by adults as a learning support to help young readers round out their knowledge of each state in the *Explore the U.S.A.* series.

Pages 4–5

Colorado's beauty inspired a famous song by Katharine Lee Bates. In 1893, she climbed to the top of Pike's Peak in the Colorado Rocky Mountains. Later, she wrote a poem that became the basis for the song "America the Beautiful." Colorado is also called the Centennial State because it became a state 100 years after the signing of the Declaration of Independence.

Pages 6–7

On August 1, 1876, Colorado became the 38th state to join the United States. Colorado is one of three states where longitude and latitude lines were used to create all of the borders. The other two are Wyoming and Utah. Seven states border Colorado. They are Wyoming, Nebraska, Kansas, New Mexico, Oklahoma, Utah, and Arizona.

Pages 8–9

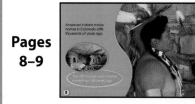

In 1904, the cave dwellings of the Anasazi Indians in McElmo Canyon were dismantled stone by stone. They were then moved by oxen and railroad to Colorado Springs. The Anasazi dwellings were reassembled at Manitou Springs. The Manitou Cliff Dwellings Museum opened in 1906. The dwellings were moved to preserve them and to protect them from vandals.

Pages 10–11

The columbine flower is native to Colorado. It is so delicate that the state has passed laws to protect the flower. The Colorado state seal uses a number of classical Roman images that represent a republican form of government. A large shield in the middle depicts three snowy mountains and a miner's tools.

Pages 12–13

Each color on the flag has a symbolic meaning. The yellow circle represents the Sun. The C stands for Colorado, and its red color represents the state's soil. The white symbolizes the snow in Colorado's mountains. The blue represents Colorado's blue skies. The flag was officially adopted in 1911.

Pages 14–15

Rocky Mountain bighorn sheep only live in the Rocky Mountains. Bighorn sheep do not shed their horns each year as other animals, such as elk or deer, do. Instead, the horns of bighorn sheep grow throughout their lives. As a result, a pair of horns can weigh up to 30 pounds (13.6 kilograms).

Pages 16–17

The state capital and largest city in Colorado is Denver. It is called the Mile High City because it is 1 mile (1.6 kilometers) above sea level. Prospectors first came to the area looking for gold in 1858, and it became a city in 1859. The city was named after James Denver, who was a governor of the Kansas Territory.

Pages 18–19

Beef is one of the top three exports from Colorado. The other two are medical instruments and aircraft parts. Colorado ranchers have raised beef cattle since the 1800s. More than 13,000 people raise more than 2.6 million cattle. In 2008, Colorado exported $500 million worth of beef to places such as Korea, China, and Japan.

Pages 20–21

Colorado is located in the Rocky Mountain range. More than 22 ski resorts are located in Colorado. One of the most famous skiing cities in the world is Aspen, Colorado. Aspen Mountain, a ski resort near the town, receives an average of 300 inches (762 centimeters) of snow every year.

KEY WORDS

Research has shown that as much as 65 percent of all written material published in English is made up of 300 words. These 300 words cannot be taught using pictures or learned by sounding them out. They must be recognized by sight. This book contains 51 common sight words to help young readers improve their reading fluency and comprehension. This book also teaches young readers several important content words, such as proper nouns. These words are paired with pictures to aid in learning and improve understanding.

Page	Sight Words First Appearance
4	and, for, is, it, its, mountains, rivers, this
7	by, in, of, other, part, states, the, where
8	American, homes, houses, Indians, made, more, moved, than, were, years
11	a, an, are, eye, has, used
15	animal, good, live, very
16	any, city, named
19	almost, each, from, makes, many, two
20	feet, go, high, people, that, to

Page	Content Words First Appearance
4	Colorado, plains
7	shape, United States
8	cliffs
11	butterflies, columbine, flower, hummingbirds, miners, nectar, pick, seal, sledgehammer, tools
12	circle, flag, Sun
15	bighorn sheep, climbers
16	capital, Denver, parks
19	cattle ranching, cows